HELP FIX CREDIT

By

Douglas Crabtree

Table of Contents

BONUS #1: REAL-WORLD TIP TO USE TOMORROW

CONCLUSION:

Introduction:

Poor credit history can prevent a person from receiving loans, credit cards and even accessing essential utilities. One must manage and repair their credit because credit cards are the third-largest source of household debt. Credit repair companies seek to support people in this scenario by extracting adverse facts from their credit records and encouraging more positive entries.

This eBook will examine the credit repair market, including the legal framework of credit report issues. Moreover, it is going to help you understand the idea behind credit repair as well as the method and tactics for taking the appropriate action on a credit report dispute. Here are some of the core topics and aspects this eBook will cover.

- Conceptual understanding of credit repair
- Credit report details
- How to increase your credit score
- Micro-payments
- Late payment entries
- Mistakes and errors in the credit report
- Tricks to tackle errors in the credit report
- Credit repair habits
- Loan issues
- Practical tips
- The proper budget planning and much more

What is Credit Repair?

It's tricky to navigate bad credit in today's contemporary society. Several firms use your credentials to determine whether to do business or trading with you and negotiate prices for the goods and services you use. So before moving ahead, you need to understand the idea of Credit Repair.

Credit repair is the method of repairing poor credit rating that may have escalated for numerous reasons. Repairing credit status can be as straightforward as disputing details about errors with credit agencies. Identity theft and the damage it causes may require some extra credit repair work. Another important aspect of credit repair is to work with critical financial problems, such as financial management, and addressing legitimate borrowers' concerns.

Usually, we equate credit repair with those who have poor credit. The reality is that at some point in their lifetime, sometimes even more than once, everybody needs to engage in credit repair. Of course, those with poor credit scores typically need it the most. So, even when you've got an average or decent ranking, you might want to raise it much more, either to increase your chances of being accepted and eligible for some loan or to get lower costs and favorable terms.

Credit repair includes two factors that we need to focus on. These factors are:

1. **Eradicating or minimizing the unfavorable entries and credit report details:**

   The process begins by getting a copy of your new credit report, then checking every line item. If any lines display negative or incriminating information, those are the ones that you want to focus on. The first objective in examining the negatives is to inspect for anything that may be in error or fault. These may involve collections that are not associated with you, records or accounts with unfavorable payment history belonging to someone else, including an ex-spouse, or open balances that you have compensated for a long time.

   So did you know that excessive credit utilization has some serious drawbacks that can weigh down your credit score? Excessive credit usage has been one of the most significant potential disadvantages, and one that is ambiguous and vague to most customers. Excessive credit usage is calculated by what's known as the percentage or ratio of credit usage. That is the total amount that you owe on your lines of credit, split by your overall credit limits.

   Okay so let's assume you have four credit cards with a $15,000 cumulative credit limit. If you owe over the four cards a minimum of $11,250, the credit utilization level is 75%. This utilization rate of 75% of the credit will be considered excessive and therefore, will drag down your credit score. Credit use is the second largest decisive factor in credit score, except for the history of payment. It contributes to about 30% of your ranking, so it is a critical mission to keep that amount at a manageable level.

2. Increase positive entries:

The increase in positive credit entries is equally essential. Often a lack of quality credit weights down a credit score. An absence of adequate credit can even hold it back. If you want a fantastic credit score, you will, of course, want to make the payments on time. Yet paying off a debt or a credit card is one of the easiest ways to boost your credit score. Moreover, you can also get extra points and increase the positive entries by paying off credit cards or an installment loan.

So, if you have poor credit, you will undoubtedly have to work to eliminate as many negative items as feasible.

Now, the reality and solution to credit repair should be quite clear. Credit repair requires correcting a bad credit rating, whether it is as easy as reporting errors or fixing certain factors due to which the evaluation might have dropped in the first place.

What is your credit score, and why do you need it?

A credit score is a figure or a number that sums up your credit reporting statistics. The scores typically vary from 300 to 850. Lenders use credit scores to determine whether you are going to repay a debt or not, and other organizations also evaluate your candidacy for a deal or a position, depending on your credit.

Here are some of the terms you need to be familiar with to understand this concept fully:

- Credit History: This is a record of your past payments of bills and other liabilities. It records all the payments that you have made and whether you made those payments within the due time or did you make late payments. It records all the payments you have not made and the amount of debt you have on you currently.

- Credit Report: This is a summary of your credit history gathered from different sources; this will help give a clearer outlook of your credit situation and whether you make your pending payments responsibly or not.

Credit score: The data in your credit report and other information about you, such as your bank statements, the property you own, and your family information are then used in a special mathematical algorithm to deduce your credit score. Also known as your FICO score, 35% of your credit score is made up of your payment history, 30% is derived from the total amount you owe currently, 15% depends on the length of your credit history, the older it is, the better and the remaining 20% is based on the mix of your credit types and new credit, which stands for the recent loan applications you have made. Your credit score has a range of 300 to 850; while scores above 700 mean good credit and above 800 are excellent, scores lower than 580 represents bad credit.

Creditors use credit scores to evaluate whether to allow you a credit card or a mortgage and what rate of interest to offer you. Organizations can also use your credit ratings to assess whether to rent a home or assign you a position or job and what to compensate for automobile insurance. Since scores have so much impact, knowing how credit scores function and the conditions that make them fluctuate is essential.

Secrets of repairing your credit score

Boosting your credit score will assist you in qualifying for lower interest rates and better terms; this also helps you to borrow money for personal purposes (a car loan, a home equity loan, a credit card, etc.) or you can purchase products, rent a property, etc. to launch or expand a business.

Credit repair is not complicated. It won't take you several months to boost your credit score. To rebuild your credit and raise your credit score, continue to follow these certain secrets and increase your ability to invest money on terms you can manage and afford.

Do you know the secret to increasing your credit score? Do you think your credit score could be a little bit better? You've already seen a large number of people on the internet talking about how they have gone through the same thing with tremendous success. So, what exactly did they implement? Do they have any magic? Or some secret tricks that you don't have? Well, yes, this might be the truth. Maybe they know these amazing tricks, and now you will know them too!

1. ## Make micro-payments

    All you need to do is to make small payments throughout the month. Micro-payments will lower your credit card's balance. You can even view your credit card as a debit card, paying electronically when an order is released. Making multiple payments over the month acts on a credit indicator called credit utilization which has a powerful impact on ratings and scores. If you can keep your usage low rather than allowing it to rise towards a payment due date, your score will gain automatically. This also cuts the interest on the account in half as you are changing the remaining balance thru out the month.

2. ## Try to higher credit limits:

    Did you know if your credit card limit rises and the balance remains the same, it will automatically lower the total use of credit? So, in such a scenario what you need to do is to contact the credit card company to inquire if you can get a higher limit without a "hard" credit inquiry, which can potentially drop a few points in your score. The higher the credit limit the more available credit you can use without going over 30%.

3. ## Dispute incorrect late-payment entries and credit report errors:

    Mistakes occur. Your mortgage lender could record a late payment which was eventually paid on time. Credit card providers can fail to register a payment correctly. You can dispute incorrect late-payment entries whether in existing or expired accounts, the very same way you question derogatory tags. Another element weighing heavily on your credit score is your payment background and history, so try hard to fix those errors. Payment history is 35% of your credit score.

4. Become an authorized user:

Find a family member or friend who has a long and responsible record of using a credit card. Ask them to add you to their credit card as an authorized user. The account owner doesn't have to allow you to use the card or make any transactions for your benefits.

5. Decide and play the game:

Okay, so let's assume that an account went to collection, you never paid or compensated it, and due to this, the collection agency decided to give up. Now all that is in your hand is the reference and entry to your credit report. In such a scenario, you can still challenge the entry. Many people do. And sometimes such issues and entries are resolved.

When you dispute the error, the credit bureau tells the agency to verify the claims and information, which a few agencies will, while others don't want to, especially collection agencies. They will completely ignore the order, and in such cases, they are required to resolve the matter and remove the entry from your credit report.

What this suggests is that smaller firms, such as collection agencies, retail borrowers or small to medium-sized providers, are much less likely to react to the credit bureaus. They don't need a headache. Banks, credit-card firms, auto finance firms, and mortgage companies are more inclined to respond. But if you do not want to use this technique, you do not necessarily have to use it. We are just suggesting that some people make decisions to use this technique. You can dispute information in the assumption that the creditor won't respond or reply. (This is the tactic that credit repair companies use to improve the ratings of their clients.) If the creditor refuses to answer, the entry is deleted.

6. Keep credit cards open

If you're trying to boost your credit profile, you should be aware that shutting down credit cards will make the job more challenging. Closing a credit card makes you lose the credit limit of that card when determining the total credit usage, which can result in a lower score. Leave the card open and periodically use it so that the provider will not lock it.

Can you improve your credit by 100?

So, if you're dealing with a lower score, you are in a better placed than anyone with a solid credit history to make gains. Now, what do you think? Does a 100-point increase sound realistic?

Did you know that the lower a person's score, the more often a 100-point increase is accomplished? That's because there's a lot of upsides and minor changes that will lead to a higher score.

And if you begin with a higher score, you probably do not need 100 points to make a significant difference with the credit products that you will get. Simply, polishing your credit will make life so much easier and give you the best chance to compete for the right terms on credit cards or mortgages.

Mistakes Can Be Made

As we have already stated, your credit report and your credit score are quite essential to you. Evaluators are humans, and human hands can make mistakes while they insert in the information provided in your credit report. You may have paid off a past-due debt, and it still comes off as overdue on your credit report. There are many kinds of things that can be wrongly represented on your credit report, so you need to take steps to fix the issues as soon as possible.

Your credit score is estimated based on your credit report's statistics and information, and they are subject to some irregularities and errors. Here's the stuff which is generally worth the trouble with the agencies to rectify:

- Credit limits stated to be less than what they are.

- Accounts that are classified as "settled", "paid negative", "paying charge-off" or anything else other than "real" or "paid as accepted" if you pay on time.
- Accounts that are still classified in bankruptcy as unpaid.
- Negative things longer than seven years (10 in the situation of bankruptcy) that should have dropped off your record automatically.

Some of the things you wouldn't care about usually include:

- Your name which is misspelled in various ways
- Obsolete or inaccurate address information
- An old employer listed as current
- The bulk of inquiries

If the name or address is misspelled due to identity fraud, or because the document has been merged with somebody else's, this should be obvious when you look at your accounts and details. You are likely to see delinquencies or statements that are not associated with you, and these should be reported immediately.

Moreover, if the credit bureau or one of the firms contributing to it is just a mess, it is typically not much to worry over. Two other things that you don't have to worry about:

- Certain accounts that you closed are classified as open.
- Closed accounts that don't claim Consumer Closed.

Closing accounts can't help and may harm your rating. Leave these alone if your primary objective is to enhance your score.

Smart ways to start building credit for the first time

Credit can be difficult to construct. It's impossible to get a deposit, a credit card or even a home if you don't have a credit history. Beginning with your first credit card so whatever you do or purchase that involves credit will automatically become a part of your credit background and history. Readout these smartest ways to build credit from scratch.

1. ## Get a secured credit card

    When you establish your credit score from scratch, you'll need a secured credit card, to begin with. A secured card is supported with a cash deposit that you make upfront; typically, the deposit balance is the same as the credit card limit. Like every other credit card, you will be using the card: to buy items, make a payment on or before the deadline, charge debt if your balance is not fully paid. Once you close your account, you will get your deposit back.

    Secured credit cards are not built to be used forever. The primary purpose of a secured card is to make your credit strong enough so that you can qualify for an unsecured card which is a card without the need for a deposit and with better benefits. ***Note, these cards are great to have only if you have a plan.*** But we will talk about that later in the reading.

2. ## Get a credit builder loan or a secured loan

    So, the sole purpose of a credit-builder is to assist people to build credit. The money you borrow is usually held by the lender in an account and will not be issued until the debt is repaid. It's a kind of a coerced saving system, and the deposits are reported to credit offices or bureaus.

    So, there is another option which says that if you have deposited money in a bank or credit union, see a secured credit-building loan. With such scenarios, the security is money in your savings or deposit certificate. Usually, the rate of interest is a bit higher than the interest you receive on the account, but it may be dramatically lower than your other options.

3. **Get a Retail Store Credit Card**

So, if you are looking for a credit card that has less strict credit requirements, you should look at Retail credit cards. As a newbie or a new credit card consumer, you will have a better chance of getting a retail credit card approved than other major varieties of credit cards.

4. **With One Credit Card**

Several first-time users of credit cards build credit card collections during their first three years of using credit. Do not fall into the trap of getting many credit cards open too early. And the more credit you have, the more you will probably wind up using it, and the tougher it will be to keep the accounts and payments in order and control. Have a plan before you apply…

Applying for multiple credit cards in a relatively short period contributes to too many credit investigations. Such inquiries can harm your credit score. Not just that, too many new credit cards can damage your credit score. It is recommended to learn how to be responsible with multiple credit cards.

5. **Pay more than the minimum on credit cards**

Did you know that your credit score doesn't affect or harm the amount of your credit card payment? your credit score takes into consideration the frequency of your payments and the money owed on your loans and credit cards. Although the amount of your payment is not reflected in your credit score, you will generally pay the balance in full every month. This will save you from bearing too much debt. If you only charge what you can afford to cover, that is not going to be an issue. Every month paying off your debt shows you're capable of paying bills, and this is precisely something investors and creditors would like to see. However, it is also a good practice to carry over a very small balance from time to time. This allows the card companies a chance to charge you interest; think of this as "I give a little to get a lot more in return".

The biggest mistakes to avoid

Prevention is better than cure. Building a good credit score is much better than fixing your credit once it has been affected or damaged. Here are some aspects you should focus on to improve your score.

1. The negative information

If negative information is on your credit report, including late payments or debt returns, it will last for seven years. To fix the damage being done to your credit, you'll need to work extra hard. You can avoid such issues by paying all of your bills on time.

2. Fail to use your credit card

So, you want a good credit score? Right? You must have at least one active account for the last six months. Moreover, if you somehow let your credit cards go unused, then it will lead to the cancellation of your account.

Well, if you want to avoid such errors, you need to use your credit card at least once every few months. This is going to keep your account active and open.

3. Too much debt or borrow

Never borrow more than you can afford. However, around 30% of your credit score is based on the debt you are carrying. So, if you have too much obligation, it can negatively impact your credit score. Another problem with borrowing more than you can manage is that it might lead to even more severe issues such as foreclosure, repossession or perhaps even bankruptcy.

4. Not maintaining check and balance

The best way to take care of your debt is to check your credit report and ratings regularly. Reviewing your credit score will help you determine where you are positioned or standing, but that does not give you the entire picture.

You should also keep an eye on your credit report and not forget to verify the accuracy of the information in it as any discrepancies may ruin your credit score. When you notice mistakes on your credit report, they can be challenged and disputed with the credit department to fix them.

Inaccuracies and errors in credit reports

You may believe your credit reports exactly mirror your credit history. But this is not always true. Mistakes and inconsistencies occur more frequently on credit reports than many people think. Many errors may be minor such as spelling errors, emails or other personal details. Many faults, such as inaccurate payment history or inserting credit accounts that do not correspond to you, could be considerably more significant.

Inaccuracies in credit reporting can occur due to data entry errors when a lender sends account information to a regional consumer credit monitoring agency. It can also happen when a user is a victim of fraud or when individuals have common names, and identical social security numbers, birth dates or residential addresses.

How can I prevent errors on my credit report?

Okay, so let's assume you've noticed some significant errors on your credit report, and you need to fix them. There are specific actions and measures you need to take to ensure the issue is resolved and eventually deleted from your report.

- The first step is to make a copy of your credit report and highlight the things you find are inappropriate.
- Send a letter to the credit bureau. Explain each issue and pursue an independent inquiry to settle the disputes. Attach all the supporting documents with the message, coding pages to suit the sections in conflicts. Never send your originals.

- Send all items by registered mail, return a submitted copy, so that you have a proof that the packet was received.
- Send a separate dispute letter to the creditor, whose declarations you do not agree with when you report the issue.
- Allude to a billing statement to find the appropriate dispute address as this is generally different from the payment address.

If your conflict includes personally identifiable information, such as your current address, enclose a copy of your driver's license or a utility bill to validate your residence. The reporting agency will launch an audit and will notify the creditors to verify whether the information is correct. If the claimant is unable to check that the entry is correct or not, this must be deleted. When the investigation is finished, and if improvements were made, the agency will give you a free copy of your report. When a mistake is detected in the audit, you are entitled to demand a revised version of your credit report be sent to all those who have obtained the report in the last six months.

Contacting the creditor first is a good idea and giving a bit of lead time before you send the complaint to the credit bureau. The claimant will presumably have rectified the mistake by the time the complaint is verified. Additionally, you can make changes remotely with the credit reporting agency. Usually, when you're on their platform, they will have links that enable you to click on a button to refute inaccurate information. You may launch an official inquiry from many online credit reports by following the links given and reviewing the disputed items as instructed. There is often no space for remarks, you will only fill out multiple-choice reasoning for each dispute or conflict. If the credit reporting agency claims the original data is accurate, they must provide you with a formal notice that specifies the person that made the final report. If you still doubt the report, launch a second independent investigation.

Whenever you are applying for credit, always make sure to provide as much personal identification detail as possible. Make sure to be careful if you want to go by a nickname but be mindful that the more name changes on your credit report, the more likely discrepancies, and errors are to arise.

Learn Responsible Credit Habits

Life can be a little uncertain. You should be ready in improving your credit score and financial fitness, it will give you freedom and stability you need for whatever life has thrown your way.

Everyone should try to be a very conscientious user of credit cards. In addition to obvious benefits like staying out of debt, highly cautious credit card users will also be healthier and less worried about their finances because they are in better control.

So, what are the core habits of highly responsible credit card users?

1. **Sign Up for Auto Pay**

   Each credit card provides an automatic system of payments. Do you know what auto pay does? It pays your bill instantly every month on the due date. Let's assume if you forgot to pay or make a late payment, this will not only lead you towards hefty fines but will also ruin your credit score. In such circumstances, you should sign up for autopay and free yourself.

   Many card companies allow you to sign up on the card's website for automatic payment; if not, contact the company and they will send you a form to fill out. Always make sure you have enough cash in your account to guarantee that you cannot get overdrawn when the auto pay enables your account withdrawal.

2. **Don't forget to register yourself on the card's website**

   Do you have online banking? If not, then you should. Whenever you sign up and register yourself for the card's website, you will be connected and get instant access to your balance on your card. Moreover, you will also get quick access to the loyalty program and customer care.

3. **Sign up for text or email notification of key events**

Nobody likes to sign into their credit card account daily or weekly due to a busy schedule. Alternatively, you can subscribe to important events such as bill due dates, etc. If you are reaching a defined spending limit, several cards will give you a reminder or a notification.

4. **Monitor your bank statement once a month**

   Even if you are registered in autopay, and you are having regular updates of your balance, this does not mean you can completely forget to review the statement. Take a deep breath and look through your account statement each month and make sure there are no misunderstood payments and bills.

5. **Avoid using all of your available credit**

   Most experts suggest that you maintain your account balance below or near the credit card limit of 30%. Okay so let's suppose you have a limit of $20,000, you need to keep a balance of less than $6,000 per month. This indicates that you are accountable and responsible for your credit and will be beneficial for your credit score. Never use more than 30% that is the Golden rule.

Pay Down Debts – Tricks and Methodologies

Are You Drowning in debt? Don't know how to get it off? The first move is to develop a plan for debt payoffs.

When you have only one debt, the strategy and tactic become quite simple. Make the most substantial monthly debt payment that you can afford and handle. Rinse, and repeat until everything is finished.

Pause for a moment to decide which kind of debt you hold. Whether it's credit card debt, student debt, consumer debt or anything else in order to evaluate how much obligation you have before you start paying back. Knowing the amount and type of your debts can bring you closer to a customized debt repayment plan.

Try the tips below if you are looking for quick ways to reduce your debt, including practical tweaks to your debt reduction plans and strategies.

- **Develop a proper plan:**

The very first step to resolve the debt crisis is to develop a plan and set a budget. For budget setting, there are many personal tools you can find online. Also, what you can do is to maintain an excel spreadsheet where you can mention your day to day and monthly expenses.

- **Next, pay off the largest and most expensive debt:** Now here comes the sorting part. What you need to do is start sorting the interest rates of your credit card from maximum to minimum interest rate. First, by clearing off the debt with the maximum interest, this is how you can increase the credit card payment at the highest annual percentage rate while continually making the minimum payment on the majority of your credit cards.

- **Pay more than the bare minimum balance:** It is a tempting thing: to only pay the lowest amount of money each month and then have the rest for yourself. This way you can delay the next payment for a month, and then you can spend the money as you like. But it is the wrong choice; paying the minimum amount not only keeps you under debt for a more extended period, but it also results in you paying more in lieu of interest and lowers your credit score. Contrarily, if you pay more than the lowest amount, you will see off the debt sooner and with a better credit score.
  Improve your ability to pay off everything by making the payments every week rather than monthly. And let's say your minimum amount is $150, now try doubling it and paying off $300 or more.

- **Halt your credit card spending:** Want to stop stacking up debt? Now disable all the credit card from your wallet and drop them at home while going for shopping or lunch. Even though you earn extra money or other bonuses by purchasing through a credit card, stop spending on your credit card till you have your budget and finance under control.

- **Use work incentives and bonuses towards debt:**
  If you are getting a work incentive during or throughout the holidays, transfer the money to your debt repayment plan. Avoid investing the incentive on a long vacation or other luxuries.

- **Remove credit card credentials from online shops:**
  When you do a lot of shopping online at one website, you may have saved your credit card information on the site to ease the purchase process. Sometimes it also ends up charging items you don't want to buy. So, if you opt for a recurring service, use a debit card provided from a major credit card service connected to your checking account.

- **Sell unnecessary goods and household items:**
  Do you have any Christmas presents or old wedding gifts gathering dust inside your cupboard? Find things you can sell online on any trusted selling platform. Do a little research to ensure that products are offered at a fair and reasonable price.

- **Adjust and modify your habits:**
  Your daily practices and activities are the reason you get into debt. Spend a little time thinking about just how you spend your money every day, every week and every month. "Why do you need your cappuccino every day? Do you think you need it? Wouldn't it be better to bring your snacks or something at lunch to work? Rather than buying unhealthy meals 3-6 times a week? Question yourself. What can I alter without losing too much of my lifestyle?

- **Award yourself for achieving goals and milestones:**
  So, if you assume your debt as a form of torture and punishment, you won't be able to pay off your debt fast. Instead, make paying off your debt a goal and praise yourself as you hit the targets of debt payouts. "The only way of paying off your credit card debt entirely is to retain it, but to do that; you must be empowered and motivated."

Establishing good credit

Establishing good credit will not happen instantly or overnight. Still, you can improve your financial background with time in several ways, starting to work on your score is never too early and the quicker you do, the happier you'll be when it gets time to purchase a house. So, read out these three helpful ways to establish good credit before you buy.

- **Check your current credit score and history:**
  Firstly, you should monitor your current credit rating and record. Each of the three monitoring agencies (Equifax, Experian, and TransUnion) provides one free credit report yearly. This reporting not only shows you where you are financially standing, but it can also illustrate any mistakes listed on your report that should always be resolved as quickly and efficiently as possible.

- **Get started early with your first line of credit:**
  When it comes to credit creation, you have to begin somewhere. Nobody is born with a great credit score it has to be developed with time. That is why getting an early start and trying to retain your very first line of credit, is important for the future.

- **Avoid massive purchases:**
  Pay attention to this if you want to buy a home. Even if you have been working hard to develop stellar credit, making large transactions of credit before and during the loan application procedure will harm the chances of loan approval. Most loan officers will tell you to not make any large credit purchases for at least 90 days before closing.

Home loan problems

Are you in a cash and finance crunch? Did you pay any of your previous loan debt dues? There are many questions, but few answers. As the property market is booming these days with property prices and interest rates for loans seeing new highs almost regularly. But is it smart on your side to sign some contract and make a profitable house offer or take-home renovation mortgage? You will need to find a suitable investor before you dive in, an investor who can assign your property the right value and appropriately finance you. Your monthly earnings and credit scores play a crucial role in determining the amount of loan you will take from any lending firm.

Twelve to fifteen-year debt repayment terms are good alternatives to larger loan amounts. The repayment period is significantly shorter than the average of 20 to 25 years. There are even debt plans with relatively fixed monthly payments, which you can pay off in thirty years, but it is a prolonged recovery period. Also, you may get yourself a deal having a low-interest rate. Many dynamic credit finance services can provide a rate cap or insurance, which can automatically eliminate any interest rate rise each year, and the interest rate on loans is paid over a limited period. You can get an appraisal to assess the value of your property as well as the closing costs that you can pay.

The applicant is expected by regular rules and regulations to provide a financial report within 3 to 4 days of receiving the loan approval. If the down payment is less than 20% of the loan balance, you are also eligible for Private Mortgage Insurance. A loan application may be issued many times for secured loans, or interest rates may rise in recent times as well as relying on the industry and business sector.

Standard mortgage loans are still very much feasible if you decide to make changes to your residence or garden landscape design. A construction loan may be given to individual lenders who wish to hire electricians, home painters, and building contractors to compensate for their contributions.

Practical tips to fix credit

Your credit score shows how you have dealt with your financial liabilities. It is based on the information from the three major bureaus. Once you have paid your credit card bills and properly handled your finances, you will get a good credit history going. On the other hand, if you have made mistakes such as not paying on time, not making the minimal payment or not paying anything at all, you will wind up with poor ratings. If you have bad ratings, you may know how hard it can be. Poor credit makes certain things more complicated, unrealistic, or costly. We all know that when banks give you a credit card or mortgage, they check your credit scores.

Credit scores being used by many financial firms ensures that when you have poor credit, the process of buying a home or car is more complicated. Also renting a place without having an excellent credit score is more challenging. Insurance carriers often charge a higher premium for drivers with poor credit ratings. Utility service providers review or pull your credit to determine if a security deposit should be paid. As times go by, the number of companies that check your credit is likely to expand, rather than diminish.

Keep in mind these tips on credit repair if you are striving towards a better credit score.

- Do not compromise accounts that are in good standing. Continue to make payments on time. NEVER MISS A PAYMENT!
- When you challenge multiple items on your credit report, just add one complaint in each letter and scatter the disputes out. The credit bureaus could become wary and frivolous for too many conflicts.
- Closing a credit card never increases your credit score. In reality, closing a credit card, particularly once the account has a balance, seems to be more likely to affect your credit rating. NEVER CLOSE ACCOUNTS IN GOOD STANDING!
- When you go through credit repair, your credit score will drop suddenly. This will not automatically mean there was something wrong. Keep adding positive information to your credit report, and this will increase your credit rating with time.
- If you have too much debt, banks are not willing to work with you, and you cannot come up with a smart solution for your monthly payment schedule; consider consumer credit counseling. This is an opportunity to get you back on track.

- When your very last option to get back on the right track is to declare bankruptcy, do not waste time on tactics that simply do not work for your situation. Find a bankruptcy lawyer and initiate that bankruptcy as soon as possible, sooner the better. Once completed you can begin rebuilding your credit and identity.

Bonus #1: Real-World Tip to Use Tomorrow
Using a credit card to establish, build or repair your credit profile with zero debt

So, this amazing real-world tip will show you how to use a credit card to establish, build or repair your credit profile with zero debt. Read this strategy below…

1. Okay now the first step is to gather all the monthly bills you have and that you normally pay with your checking or debit card such as: Electric, Cable, Cell Phone, Internet access, Auto Insurance, etc.
2. Compare all the bills and pick the smallest bill you have. Now start with that bill like- the mobile or cell phone bill, or etc. It will help you understand how this works first before you further expand the methodology.
3. Pick one credit card and mark it or label it "just mobile phone bill only", but make sure that this credit card's limit is at least four times higher than the actual amount of the bill. So, let's say your cell phone bill is $100, the credit card limit should be $400 or more.
4. Now at last what you need to do is to leave your cash or money in your account. Now you are going to begin using your credit card to pay for your mobile phone and take the money in your account to pay for your credit card. Do this before the end of your credit cards' billing cycle ends so you pay zero in interest. Now, by implementing this, you are creating new credit history with a credit card, pay no interest using the card, and you are never using more than 25% of your total

available credit line. Your payment history is 35% of your total credit profile so this is Key.

5. Use this method and implement it to as many bills as you want to increase your payment history on your profile. The more you have the better your profile will be. All done without creating more debt…

Conclusion:

In summary, if you follow the tips, we have just discussed in this eBook you will find an increase in your credit rating in a short period of time. A good credit score is critical in modern financial affairs and is needed for getting loans and other matters to go through smoothly. No secrets: just using tools in a different way to get the results you want. If you are already suffering from poor credit, establishing your credit repair plan using tips in this eBook will help you re-establish the credit quality and credit score that can provide you with the best possible interest rates. Enjoy!!!